BLOODTHIRSTY FOR M.

Susannah Dickey is the author of two previous pamphlets, *I had some very slight concerns*, and *genuine human values*, both published by The Lifeboat. Her first novel, *Tennis Lessons*, will be published in July 2020 by Doubleday.

bloodthirsty for marriage

Published by Bad Betty Press in 2020
www.badbettypress.com

Cover design by Amy Acre

Printed and bound in the United Kingdom

A CIP record of this book is available from the British Library.

ISBN: 978-1-913268-07-7

Supported using public funding by
ARTS COUNCIL ENGLAND

LOTTERY FUNDED

bloodthirsty
for
marriage

PRESS

bloodthirsty for marriage

Contents

Introduction

In an early scene of *Muriel's Wedding* (1994), Muriel is ostracized by her peers in a cocktail bar called Breakers. Tania, one of the primary antagonists, has discovered that her new husband, Chook, has been receiving fellatio from another woman. Flanked by two of her blithe associates, Tania delivers the line:

I'm a bride! I'm supposed to be euphoric!

In her delivery, 'bride' goes stressed, 'I'm' unstressed, and 'supposed' unstressed stressed, placing, at the heart of this 11 syllable line, a choriamb, an early distinguishing marker of the hendecasyllable.

In his writing on the origin of hendecasyllables, the critic George Lafaye says this of the character of the genre, regarding the place it held in Roman writing: 'No kind of verse except comic trimeter was more like prose. It lacked dignity.' According to the critic, the law of the form requires the poet to trample underfoot all modesty, and of several accusations levied at hendecasyllables, two were:

1. If poetry itself was frivolous, what could they think of a man who gave his time to the most frivolous kind of poetry?
2. The hendecasyllable gave too much attention to love affairs, which are dangerously enervating to men.[1]

---

1. Hack, R. K. "The Law of the Hendecasyllable." Harvard Studies in Classical Philology, vol. 25, 1914, pp. 107–115.

This pamphlet takes its name from *Muriel's Wedding*, and the poems employ a corrupted version of the hendecasyllable, drawing on, among others, the narratives of Hero and Leander, Heloïse and Abelard, Constance Spry, Isaac and Abraham, Shergar, Achilles and Patroclus, Reinette and Mirabelle, and Saint Agatha of Sicily.

An additional note: in English poetry, the term 'hendecasyllable' has been used to describe a line of iambic pentameter with a feminine ending.

[message withdrawn]

So many buildings in the fog. They drifted
in and out of clarity like a Britpop
single like a newly shorn old memory.
They had columns and the clouds were pink cream brown.
Neapolitan cumulonimbus. Once
I wrote a song to help me remember all
the types of clouds. It was the same tune I used
for all my songs. I can't remember it now.
Why are you telling me this? the bird that lives
at the corner of my mouth asks and I have
no answer. The bird moderates my actions
but I choose never to resent it. You know
my proclivity for sentimentalism
I tell the bird That's why you arbitrate so
harshly. The bird calls me frankenfood it wants
to wear me as a hat. It whittles me down
to little terracotta strips it chews on
my tongue like a Gaviscon. [The bird is small
the bird is black and the bird is not a small
blackbird.] The bird tells me that my memories
are false memories are unreliable.
Columns it says Haven't been fashionable
for years. The clouds looked like the hands of people
struggling I say Like a sack violent with
meristems. This is a funeral the bird
says Have some respect [so I have some respect]
But not too much respect the bird says. I cried

once on top of someone but it might have been
an affectation. The sky is the colour
scheme of a couscous salad. The bird will eat
the sourdough when it decides I've had enough.
[I barely know the man in the coffin but
he had a name like the first flower to come
back to Hiroshima.] At night I pull all
the erroneous hairs from my body lay
them like cirrus feathers. Thank you for this my
hassium suffering I say. Soon I will
consume the bird. It will in turn consume me.

expanding and contracting

On the porch of the jalopy beach house by
the windblown North Antrim coast I'm the antique
rocking chair. The salt air settles in my grains
and when my grandchildren visit they haunt me
[this is my new christ metaphor bring me seed
oil bring me sundried tomatoes]. That tree once
housed invasive species. The chain went hyrax
python falcon and they made their homes within
one another. Now I'm the well-trod welcome
mat. The salt air damps my cilia. [Something
we like to say is that everyone has been
the fly in an ointment or the horseshoe in
a margarita.] The sun leaks pleasantly
onto the sea's marble countertop. [Enter
a woman conspicuous and likable.]
She watches the sky melt and says I wasn't
expecting this. [But maybe she should have been.]
She has milk teeth in an old old mouth. You know
she says You know if everything good must turn
bad I'm thrilled this is how it goes about it.

a black cloth over your face isn't the same as night

I used up the summer controlling people
[in a video game]. I made him handsome
and tall and I made her patent the peanut
-size sheath that keeps umbrellas open that keeps
them from collapse. She got picked up for work in
a mint green Datsun each morning and one day
I made him drop his soft wallet in the street
and I made her DING DING hurtle after him
like a sneeze. I watched their nailless fingers touch
and then I intervened because god! think of
a pursuit less fruitful than affinity!
I made them go about their days. He married
a dentist and she died young and he ran down
his years evading the diagnoses of
bruxism and she died young. Neither handed
the damp debasement of a life spent wanting.
Their lives were lilac aldehyde there was no
asbestos slung behind their walls. Now Autumn

is here and I need a life soft-edged with heart
motif a small girl's ring-bound notebook. I need
insight. It oozes from the corners navy
damp DING DING You're a product of your choices
you're a totem pole you're hunger on top of
caprice on top of the grazed cheeks of debauched
nights spent folded your face in the gravel like
an animal. I decide to fix things I
streamline my practices. I wear a yellow
mini dress in an always temperate clime.
My house is pristine now and if not I'll eat
or fuck or swim to lessen the scores of it
all. I'll buy a dog and then I'll teach that dog
to die and when it does my children will be
prepared for everything in the world and then
– when my life is panacea smooth – a new
person will enter the game through the back door
DING DING yes it is attainment and we'll dance.
We'll dance to the open fire on the stove
top to the graceless wordless music to all
the things I mistook for the sky and we'll dance
to the entombed cockatoo moans of my dog
– buried neat beneath the geranium bush.

good career move

She sits on small Slemish's horizontal
grass. A collapsed tent with her peeled lychee skin.
Everything lies new on her like a pasta
bake glow. I've bound her hands and feet with knotted
together sports socks and the first thing she asks
me is if they're clean. [Look. Those upturned smoosh cheeks.]
Getting older is just remembering all
that has been demanded of you I tell her.
[I can see the shadow of a much smaller
bull. There's a yellow knife in my pocket.] I
wonder why I needed the mountain at all.
But oh. Yes. The wind on my scalp I remind
myself. People have stopped asking about my
plans and it's raining [in that way where it comes
from inside you]. This is what having your foot
in the door of hopelessness is I tell her.
If anyone asks I'll say god told me to.
If anyone asks I'll say god told me not
to. [This venison neck. This recurring rage.]

stained glass folklore

The world's tics will modulate the bokeh skin
of coloured glass. [A triangle of birds throws
linseed across it. Autumn sky's different
from summer sky.] A woman goes to Castle
-dawson and forks out for a stained glass window
at auction. A big St. Agatha hiding
her freggio'd chest with a black egg. It gets
abandoned in the oubliette basement of
The Lucky Harbringer pub it promptly forms
a lean-to against stacked boxes of Scampi
Fries™. [Yellow glass stain came like a well
-timed inheritance cheque it brought the turning
of blue green of white yellow. It made peasants
into young sexy peasants and saints into
young sexy saints.] The woman once had butter
-toned hair and people said she looked heavenly.
Now she makes it yellow with pharmacy-grade
ammonia. She looks like a pale fire
escape in lingerie and she's pale frightened
of punchlines. Still. All women are ingénues
of the school of worrying about their age.
One night she goes down to change the empty kegs.
[The underside of a pub is a lot like
the underside of a church organ its throats
drone sonorous.] She finds Agatha exposed.
The black egg open crocus-like on the floor.

St. Agatha blinks – Oh! – and the blue pliers
in her hand masticate wildly and her chest
is meatless [scored as a cheeseboard]. The woman
blinks too – Oh! – is renewed and for the first time
she thinks peaceably of her dead husband of
the opal china elephant she bought him
in an antique store. He used it to hold his
car keys so one night she took both and buried
them in the garden. In the damp earth they formed
a fresco – the key fob a blob tank ready
to battle the elephant gentle cosmic
as breast milk and all the while he was upstairs
dying in a chair. When she found him her hair
turned colourless. Normal days are the hardest
St. Agatha says Normal is a fridge door
slamming over and over while you try to
thread a needle and god! the weight of it would
just knock you over. The woman curls up at
St. Agatha's feet. She holds wet flakes of old
eggshell like corsages. She is a paisley
teardrop. She is a seed-shaped vegetable.

there were things I was just too lazy to tell you

Everything is on fire and everyone
is on fire. AHHHHH the people say AHHHHHH AHHHHHHH.
The fire starts among the smallest mammals
– gerbils hamsters dwarf mice the ones the people
kept as ornaments. It was thought not to be
pass on-able but still their tiny eyelashed
bodies were sought out and destroyed their screams thick
as soot. Then the fire mutated [as most
things do eventually] and it settled
on bare skin and it ripped through Altnagelvin's
cotton neonatal units and baguette
geriatric units. Men with scorching sores
sat on corners shaking tins. They'll only spend
it on drink I heard someone say. Boo to you
piss off Janine I thought. There's no cure after
all – what would we have them do? I find you pale
-skinned in a bambi glade far from Derry's streets
and riots and fires. We hold each other
like office. We watch a helicopter limp
through the sky – its hose swinging like a sperm whale's
dick its pilot engulfed. We lie still blissful
in our immunity. You feel warm. But then
you always did. [You're hot baby you're a straight
up smokeshow.] It's then that I see the birthday
candle flames leaking from your sock and you try
desperately to blow them out. I thought I
was special you say. The tear evaporates

on reaching your cheek. I thought I was something
different you say. Above a formation
of geese crimson moulting tears the sky in two.
Your form wilts – the hem of your trousers smoking.
I roll up my sleeve and show you the soft knob
of my wristbone the way the scalloped yellows
and reds circle it like acolytes. I thought
I was special too I say and you hold me
tighter. Not long now I say. Our skin sputters
with the sound of a hundred breaking wishbones.

remove the oboe and joy will follow

After 'Leander and Hero' by Hannah Lash

It comes in a fur-lined case like a well-cared
for recently deceased firearm. It comes
with its own screwdriver [smaller than any
regular screwdriver]. Why are kids always
being given small versions of regular
things and asked to consider them toys? Come. Get
ready – you're now the mechanic of something.
When an oboe gets blown it's a chorus of
the throat and it's a slow and ancient courtship
and it's a clown car horn. An oboe will make
Debussy's Little Shepherd an asymptote.
It makes Sloop John B a bit doughy and it
makes its player wet and undignified [low
C or high E flat is three UTIs at
once]. This is because the oboe is a witch
finger a regular man's store-bought ginger
stem. The oboe will take you to the forefront
of an orchestra's mind where it sighs mohair
loneliness. The oboe decides to wake you
with the clamminess of its unplayedness. It
puts you in spaces that need to be filled but
it doesn't make you interesting. It's not
enough to recuse you from your decisions
it's not a baby or a glass eye. A dead
relative of historical relevance.
The oboe [brought out and shown off] is a gasp.
It's breath held separate. It's the damp whistling
holes across Wabakimi Provincial Park.

21

all lovely tales

1.0 And in this version I decide to find him

ten years from now on a university
polygon campus. He's turning Mondrian

windows into daguerreotypes with his grey
jacket and grey hairs. Meanwhile I'm walking with

a cane [limping prettily as Heloïse
but of course he doesn't realise.] He takes

me to a union rally and his public
hands wrapped around my all too public waist rule

out the possibility of promotion.
That night in a lamp lit office [my newly

older skin lumpy like radiator skin
like brushed sesame toast] we pace like ferrets.

I open clandestinely to the last page
in a book of translations. [It brings me such

filthy pleasure to gatekeep knowledge.] 19th
century Polish poetry and a prose

poem boxy as a tax return. Two frogs
caught in a clear terrarium forced to live

out a heterosexual suburban
dreamscape. Evening frog it says Charmed frog freshen

your drink frog yes please frog of course frog oh god
make me your open legs sexy dirty wife

frog. [Maybe this is what he wanted when we
met.] I read the poem's final lines in night

-ripe whispers sexy as a blow-up mattress
[Oh! Selenicereus grandiflorus].

Tisk tisk the Woman Frog thought I suspected
this happiness wasn't for the likes of us.

2.0 and in this version [voice capri pant sweet] see

the macaroons' pink dollops of cartilage.
[Their inner places are hard parabolas.]

I stand by a loaded lace tablecloth and
wish I was a French nun. As things stand I shall

probably never be French. Shall never be
a nun. So much good stuff is out of reach on

birth. Look – the academic pouring slaked lime
into his tea will get castrated. The mob

who castrates him will also get castrated.
Castration is a soft tray of dominos.

Look! these domino finger sandwiches – prawn
exoskeletons and wet grape pheromones.

Funeral vol-au-vents and white sausages.
When I die my remains will reignite this

place's one-time popularity. I seek
out rain. Pain follows like a credit rating.

2.1 and in this other version I'm late for this

recital running humid across the snail
-juiced roads. I whisper sorry to the foyer
columns. I want to label them S and P.
I want to turn this place on its fat belly
like Carthage. Each gesture wastes the pianist
more – his arpeggio'd biceps turning to
semolina. Desire will knit your flat
world's ends together he says If only it
also deposited you memory-less
in a fjord. I take the backstreets home. I put
my hands in an empty freezer so they feel
less like an inheritance that I've wasted.

2.2 and in this sticky chlorophyllic version

I buy a cheesecake in a South Bank café.
There are three layers to it and it goes brown

then dark yellow then light yellow. The rumoured
summer has come and there are tits on display

it's horrible and it's lovely and people
on this fake beach are writing love messages

in the sand. The graphic of a v-shaped heart
between initials turns a relationship

into a court proceeding. Across the slabs
of the veranda a woman is turning

to ash on a plastic chair. Her ears and arms
dandruffing off rude as confessions and all

over her skin skate parks are being carved out.
[Her teeth turn eroded limestone her mouth sings

out like a tuning fork.] By the time this scraped
-empty cheesecake tub makes its discarded way

to the bin to the sewers to the chalky
river to the manmade shore the woman will

have disappeared and probably R and K
– S and S – won't be together anymore.

It's so easy to ignore things when it's like
this a cry for help is gum on a pavement

when it's like this. A breeze will carry her off
soon. Nothing left but her jeans knickers sandals.

What might seem like a big event to a small
life needn't be all that big you know? She'll be

gone soon and that's alright. She'll be mistaken
for detritus dropped bits of old cheesecake and

that's alright. I think H and L might make it
you know. They always were the best of us. Look.

The Thames moves like dialysis. In this light
just about anyone can be beautiful.

3.0 and in this version [all my rich side projects]

I'm crouched in a dank cupboard with a fibre
optic Christmas tree and a woman convinced

it's World War Two. She pushes spaghetti hoops
to her mouth with bloody mud-curated hands

listens to the soundlessness of imagined
air raids. Something is afoot she says. Something

is a leg I say Or something is a hand
because generosity of spirit died

recently after an extended bout of
illness. We lost many good men in the field

she says. It must have been a fucking big field.
Empty gloves drop from the mallard's neck night sky.

3.1 and in this recent version [epilogue joy]

I might take you to a party introduce
you to all my bright party friends. Be wary
at first they might be suspicious of you – one
chomping at a lobster's skull to assert his
dominance. Forget them. You never told a
woman she's responsible for your living
bearably. They can tell. You never threatened
to die at her and they don't know what to do
with that. You are blue so blue Amalfi blue
a revolution blue. So listen – I won't
begrudge you your manness but there were four men
before you who forced me to do exactly
that. I always go to costume parties dressed
as a snake in a Hot Wheels box but what's weird
is that under it all I'm actually
a worm. I am a great hulking party worm
and these men were my party worm friends. I loved
them all so desperately. Listen – my high
altitude lozenge. I promise I once had
reasons – good reasons! – to go to the airport.

3.2 and in this version I invent a dish called

coronation chicken and I bring roses
fat and opulent back to fashion. Loving

a man is always a miasma I tell
Rosemary. She ignores me hides my bookends

below an armchair. I agree they don't fit
the aesthetic and one hour later I die

falling down this ornate Easter egg staircase.
My last words are Someone else can arrange this.

—·—

I could have been loved. Just barely. I could have
loved. Like a stain. Maybe. If I hadn't let

things be taken. If I hadn't given things
away. I'm always aching these glass years since.

My wardrobe's full of pleather and bandages.
A suit made from wet dog hair and oestrogen.

Life goes pain pain pain mutable pain joy pain.
Good god I'm still here. Miraculous. I guess.

4.0 and in this version [ending the feminine]

I'm full of war as an unfed gull. Watch me
wear the head of someone more beautiful and
frightening than me and throw myself onto
a battlefield. [The head fits like Pasiphaë's
maternity pants.] Three testudine years have
passed and I find him in this campus bathroom
shampooing stains from his suit jacket senseless
and lambent. It's his only suit he tells me.
His face grey his hair grey and the glaucous wool
the greyest I've seen. The shampoo bottle sits
on the sink top pomegranate-effusive.
I plunge my hands into wet and make the ripe
stains of red wine blush. [He wears his palpable
sadness like Munich. I don't get it.] My in
-ternal and external voices recently
became one [which isn't to say I express
myself any better or more frequently].
I don't want to be older he says I want
to be rid of all this damn hope. We'll spend two
more years in this syllabub room rubbing plant
extracts on wounds listening for the crackle
of futility [dirt under skin]. I want
to be orphaned of desire then orphaned
of ambition. I'm furious everyone
is watching me become ugly. We'll spend six
more months here – till there's no suit jacket and till
there never was a suit jacket and till there's
nothing. And in this version there's nothing. Just
foam. Just pink. [The cistern's moan.] Just miscreance.

I have a reason for asking but I'd rather not share

A beloved and famous race horse was found
shot. Its legs were stiff and pointed at the sky
and in the grainy photos in the local
paper it resembled a toast rack. It was
buried in a hollowed grand piano just
large enough to accommodate its body.
The body of the piano – the shape of
a sock puppet in use – was lined with fur and
a child – I don't know who she belonged to – tugged
my arm and asked Will he still get to race in
heaven? and I said – because it was raining –

Horses don't go to heaven. What are you – stupid?

Notes and acknowledgements

I am grateful to the editors of the following journals and
anthologies, for publishing early versions and misshapen cousins of
these poems: *Ambit*; *The White Review*; *The Scores*; *Hotel*; *The Rialto*;
On Relationships (3 of Cups Press, 2020); 'Happy Browsing': An
Anthology in Praise of Bookfinders (The Tangerine, 2018).

Thank you to Amy and Jake at Bad Betty. Thank you to Stephen
Connolly and Manuela Moser at The Lifeboat, for believing in the
hefty long poem. Thank you to Will Harris, for being a considerably
more generous reader than I had any right to expect. Thank you to
the writers at the Seamus Heaney Centre, Belfast, for helping me
count syllables.

New and recent titles from Bad Betty Press

poems for my FBI agent
Charlotte Geater

No Weakeners
Tim Wells

The Body You're In
Phoebe Wagner

Blank
Jake Wild Hall

*And They Are Covered
in Gold Light*
Amy Acre

Alter Egos
Edited by Amy Acre
and Jake Wild Hall

She Too Is a Sailor
Antonia Jade King

Raft
Anne Gill

While I Yet Live
Gboyega Odubanjo

The Death of a Clown
Tom Bland

Forthcoming in 2020

At the Speed of Dark
Gabriel Akamo

War Dove
Troy Cabida

Animal Experiments
Anja Konig

A Terrible Thing
Gita Ralleigh

Sylvanian Family
Summer Young

Rheuma
William Gee

Lightning Source UK Ltd.
Milton Keynes UK
UKHW010849030720
365936UK00004B/354